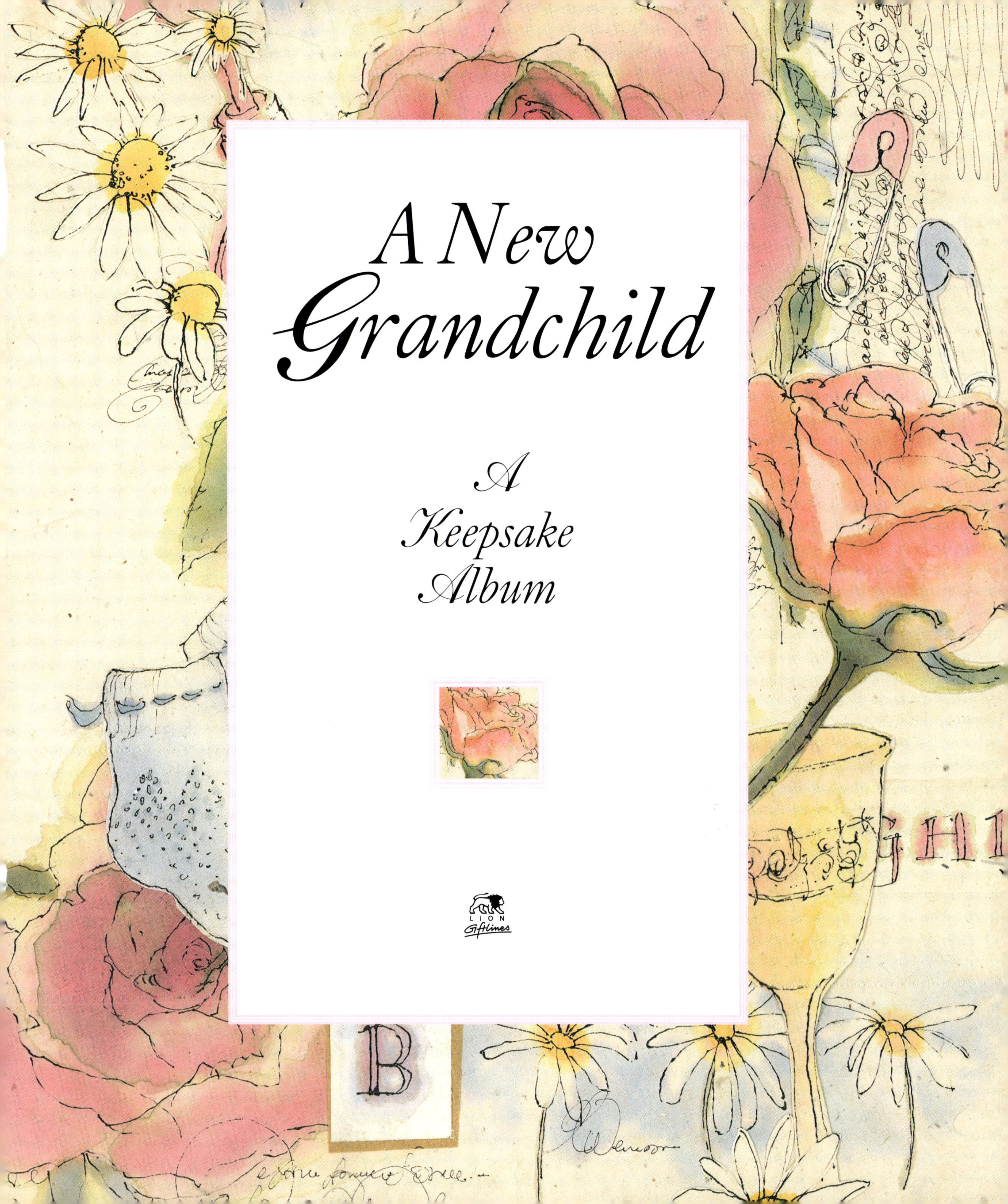

A New Grandchild

A Keepsake Album

LION Giftlines

Published by
Lion Publishing plc
Sandy Lane West, Oxford, England
ISBN 0 7459 3988 0

First edition 1998
10 9 8 7 6 5 4 3 2 1 0

Acknowledgments
We would like to thank all those who have given us permission to include quotations in this book. Every effort has been made to trace and acknowledge copyright holders. We apologize for any errors or omissions that may remain, and would ask those concerned to contact the publishers, who will ensure that full acknowledgment is made in the future.

A catalogue record for this book is available from the British Library

Printed and bound in Singapore

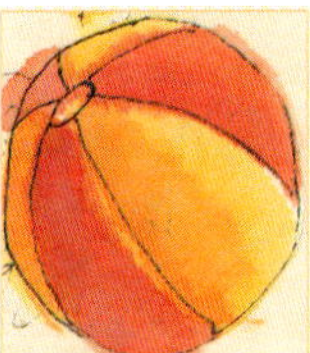

Introduction

Becoming a grandparent can give rise to a whole host of feelings: joy at the wonder of a new life, love for this latest family member – all mixed together with a deep sense of responsibility and a recognition of the inevitable passing of time. What many grandparents relish is the opportunity to really enjoy their grandchild – free from the normal day-to-day concerns of parenthood itself.

And this is indeed a very special relationship: one in which the wisdom of the years can be shared with a new generation, and where small things can be enjoyed together – often at a much more leisurely pace. As one small child chirped: 'Everybody should try to have a grandparent, especially if you don't have a television, because they are the only grown-ups who have time.'

Being a grandparent presents a wonderful opportunity to love, cherish and support not only your grandchild, but also your own child. It doesn't matter if distance is a factor; modern communications mean that contact may be only a phone call or a letter away.

Whether you live near or far, this keepsake album will enable you to record the special events and milestones in your grandchild's life – from the day of birth through the early years of childhood. There is space for you to write about times you've spent together or been in touch, and to make a note of specific details about your grandchild's development. And you can paste photographs or other mementoes of special moments: perhaps a first painting, or a card or letter you have received.

You can use this album exactly as you wish – it is yours to make your own! In doing so, you will give expression to a unique life – and a unique relationship. And this, together with the quotations and reflections provided, will also give a real sense of family, of continuity and of love, both human and divine.

Family tree

Great-grandfather

Great-grandmother

Grandfather

Great-grandfather

Great-grandmother

Grandmother

Great-grandfather

Great-grandmother

Grandfather

Great-grandfather

Great-grandmother

Grandmother

Father

Baby

Mother

Welcome!

What a happy day! A day to rejoice in the moment – and to treasure precious memories of when your own child was born. Here is space for you to record details and paste photographs or other mementoes of the birth of your grandchild.

Name

Date and time of birth

Place of birth

Weight

Height

Colour of eyes

Colour of hair

Photographs / Mementoes

Children are a gift from the Lord;
they are a real blessing.

From Psalm 127 (GNB)

Photographs / Mementoes

Getting to know you

These pages are for you to remember the first time you met your grandchild – perhaps in the hospital, or at home. This day is one to treasure; it is surely the beginning of a new journey.

Date

Place

Photographs / Mementoes

We define the soul
as born of the
breath of God.

Tertullian

At Christmas-time

Christmas is such a joyful time, especially when filled with the laughter and excitement of babies and children. You can use these pages to record memories of your grandchild at Christmas-time: perhaps baby's first Christmas, times spent together, gifts given and received.

Date

Place

It is good to be children sometimes, and never better than at Christmas, when its mighty founder was a child himself.

Charles Dickens

Photographs / Mementoes

A special day

Many parents choose to mark their baby's arrival with a public ceremony - perhaps a church service or a family party. This is a time for friends and relations to join together in celebration of and commitment to a unique life. Here you can record the details of your grandchild's special day.

Date

Occasion

Place

Guests

Photographs/ Mementoes

Photographs

Children need the wisdom of their elders;
the ageing need the encouragement of a
child's exuberance.

Unknown

The first year

Special moments

These pages are for you to record special times you have spent with your grandchild during the first year, using words, photographs and mementoes.

Photographs / Mementoes

Love makes everything lovely.

George Macdonald

Happy first birthday!

Use these pages to record details and paste photographs of your grandchild's first birthday. Note down your thoughts and feelings at this time.

Date

Celebration

Guests

Gifts

Special memories

Photographs

Milestones

Here is space for you to record some of the milestones and details of your grandchild's first year.

Weight at age one

Height at age one

First smiled

First laughed

First reached out for objects

First 'words'

First sat up alone

First crawled

First stood up alone

Favourite food

Favourite games

Favourite toys

Favourite friends

Other details

Photographs

Photographs

Grandparents need grandchildren to keep the changing world alive for them. And grandchildren need grandparents to help them know who they are and to give them a sense of human experience in a world they cannot know.

Margaret Mead

The second year

Special moments

These pages are for you to record special times you have spent with your grandchild during the second year, using words, photographs and mementoes.

Photographs / Mementoes

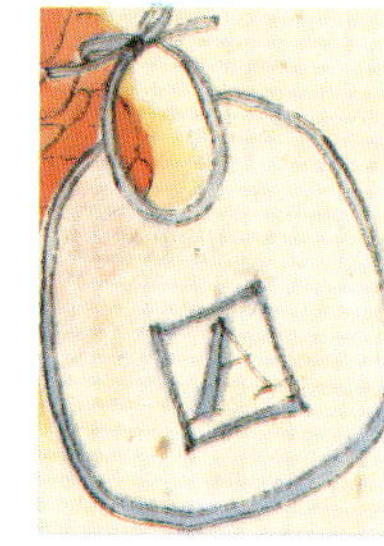

One laugh of a child will make
the holiest day more sacred still.

Robert G. Ingersoll

Happy second birthday!

Use these pages to record details and paste photographs of your grandchild's second birthday. Note down your thoughts and feelings at this time.

Date

Celebration

Guests

Gifts

Special memories

Photographs

Milestones

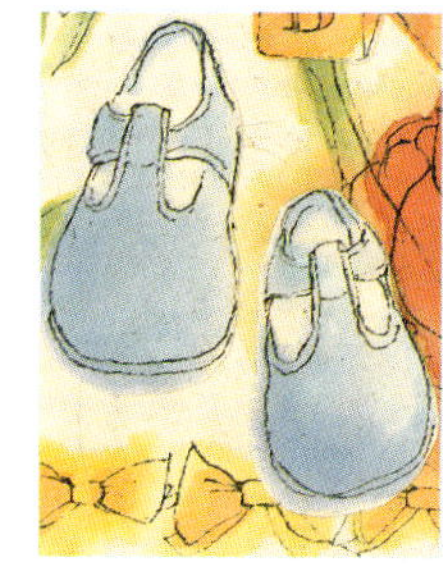

Here is space for you to record some of the milestones and details of your grandchild's second year.

Weight at age two

Height at age two

First walked

First 'ate' alone

First painting

First kicked a ball

First 'sentence'

Favourite food

Favourite games

Favourite toys

Favourite friends

Other details

Photographs

Photographs

Have great care of your children…
Teach them to love truth.

Macarius of Optino

The third year

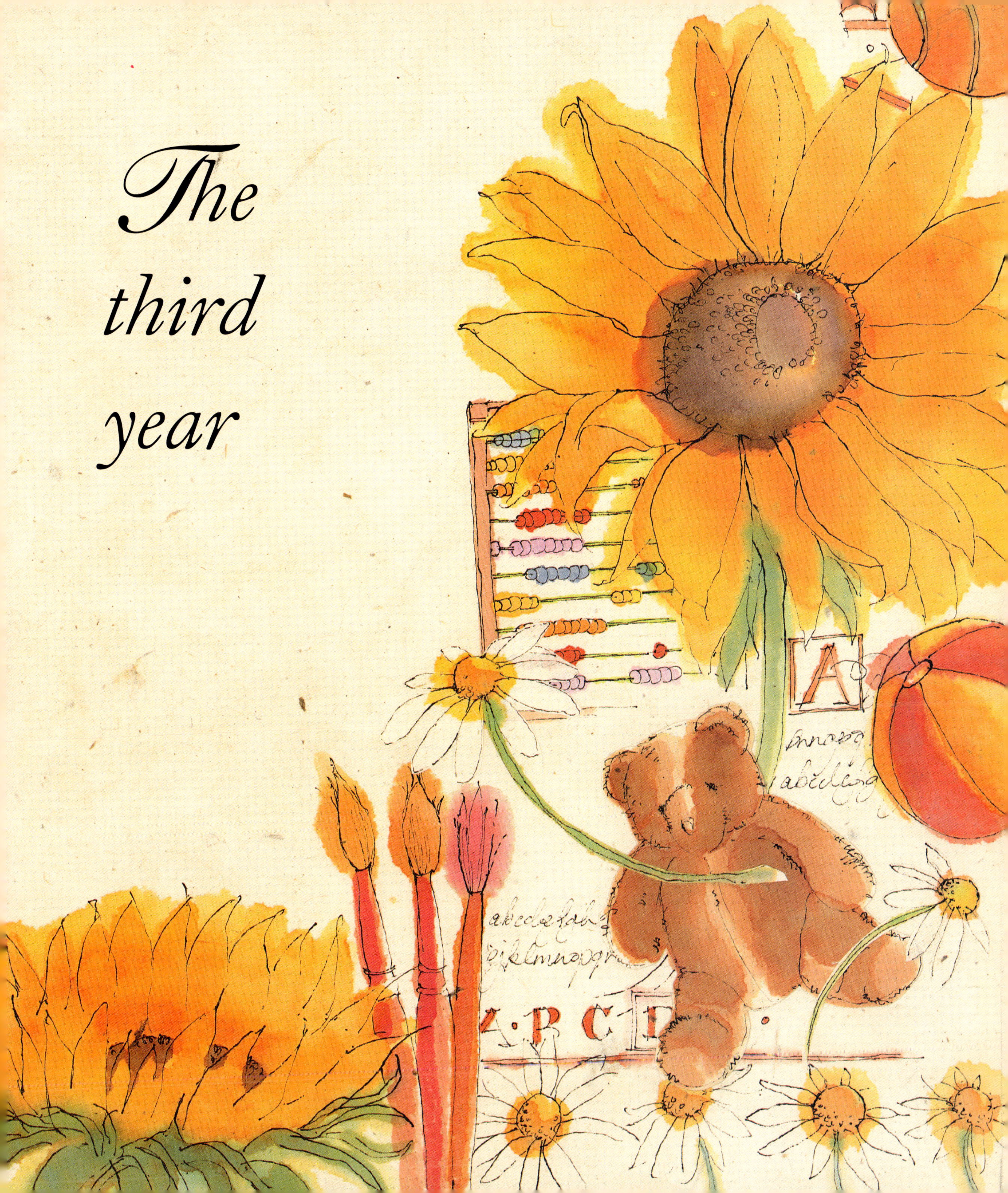

Special moments

These pages are for you to record special times you have spent with your grandchild during the third year, using words, photographs and mementoes.

Photographs / Mementoes

From a little spark may
burst a mighty flame.

Dante Alighieri

Happy third birthday!

Use these pages to record details and paste photographs of your grandchild's third birthday. Note down your thoughts and feelings at this time.

Date

Celebration

Guests

Gifts

Special memories

Photographs

Milestones

Here is space for you to record some of the milestones and details of your grandchild's third year.

Weight at age three

Height at age three

First rode a tricycle

First went to playgroup

Favourite food

Favourite rhymes and songs

Favourite stories

Favourite games

Favourite toys

Favourite friends

Other details

Photographs

Photographs

Jesus took the children in his arms,
put his hands on them and blessed them.

Adapted from the Gospel of Mark

The fourth year

Special moments

These pages are for you to record special times you have spent with your grandchild during the fourth year, using words, photographs and mementoes.

Photographs / Mementoes

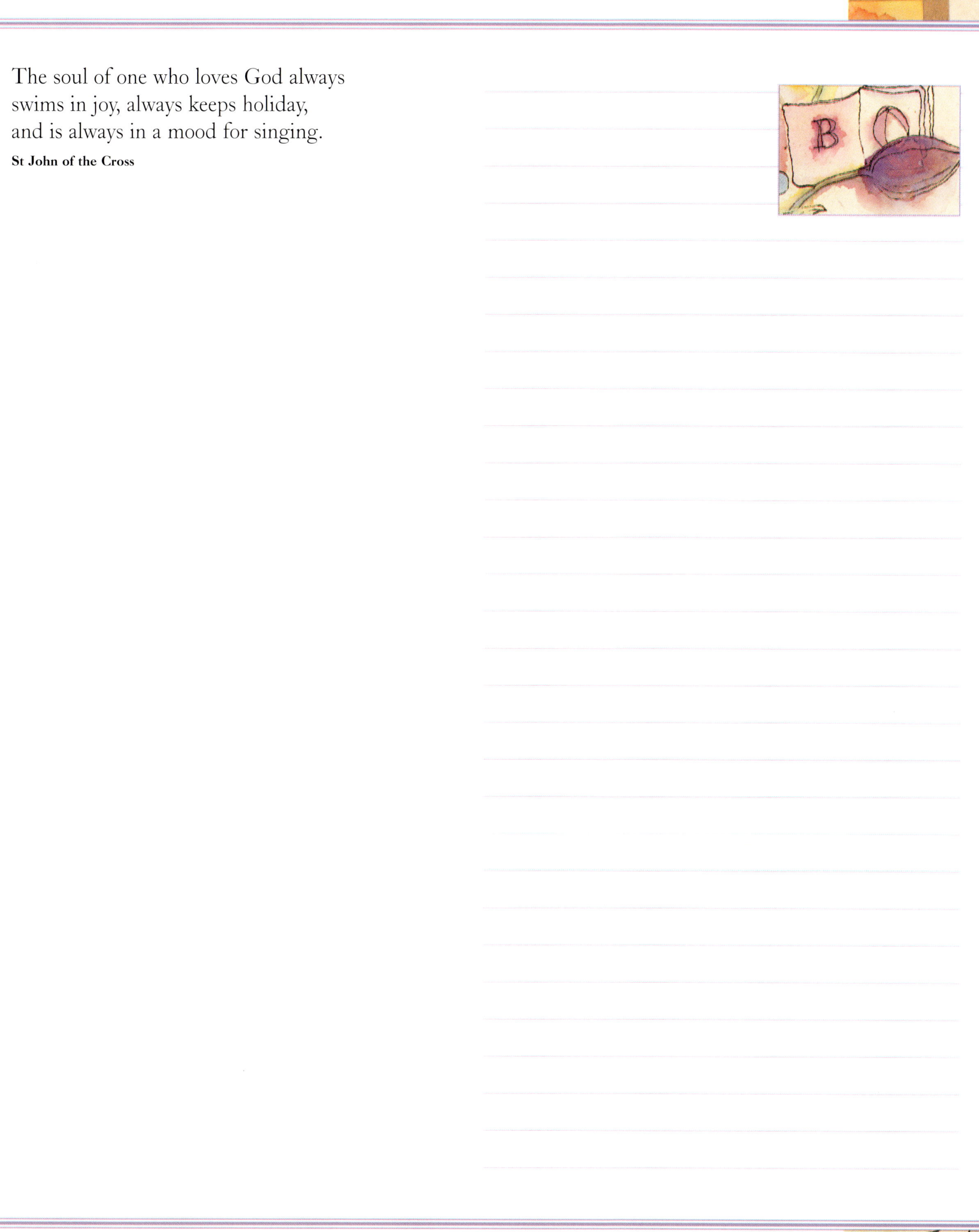

The soul of one who loves God always
swims in joy, always keeps holiday,
and is always in a mood for singing.

St John of the Cross

Happy fourth birthday!

Use these pages to record details and paste photographs of your grandchild's fourth birthday. Note down your thoughts and feelings at this time.

Date

Celebration

Guests

Gifts

Special memories

Photographs

Milestones

Here is space for you to record some of the milestones and details of your grandchild's fourth year.

Weight at age four

Height at age four

First used a knife and fork

First went to nursery school

Favourite food

Favourite rhymes and songs

Favourite stories

Favourite games

Favourite toys

Favourite friends

Other details

Photographs

Photographs

Grandchildren are the crown of the aged.

From Proverbs 17 (RSV)

The fifth year

Special moments

These pages are for you to record special times you have spent with your grandchild during the fifth year, using words, photographs and mementoes.

Photographs / Mementoes

I am so happy, I am so happy.

Gerard Manley Hopkins

Happy fifth birthday!

Use these pages to record details and paste photographs of your grandchild's fifth birthday. Note down your thoughts and feelings at this time.

Date

Celebration

Guests

Gifts

Special memories

Photographs

Milestones

Here is space for you to record some of the milestones and details of your grandchild's fifth year.

Weight at age five

Height at age five

First went to school

Favourite food

Favourite rhymes and songs

Favourite stories

Favourite games

Favourite toys

Favourite friends

Other details

Photographs

How you have changed!

First week

Six months old

One year old

Eighteen months old

Two years old

Three years old

Four years old

Five years old

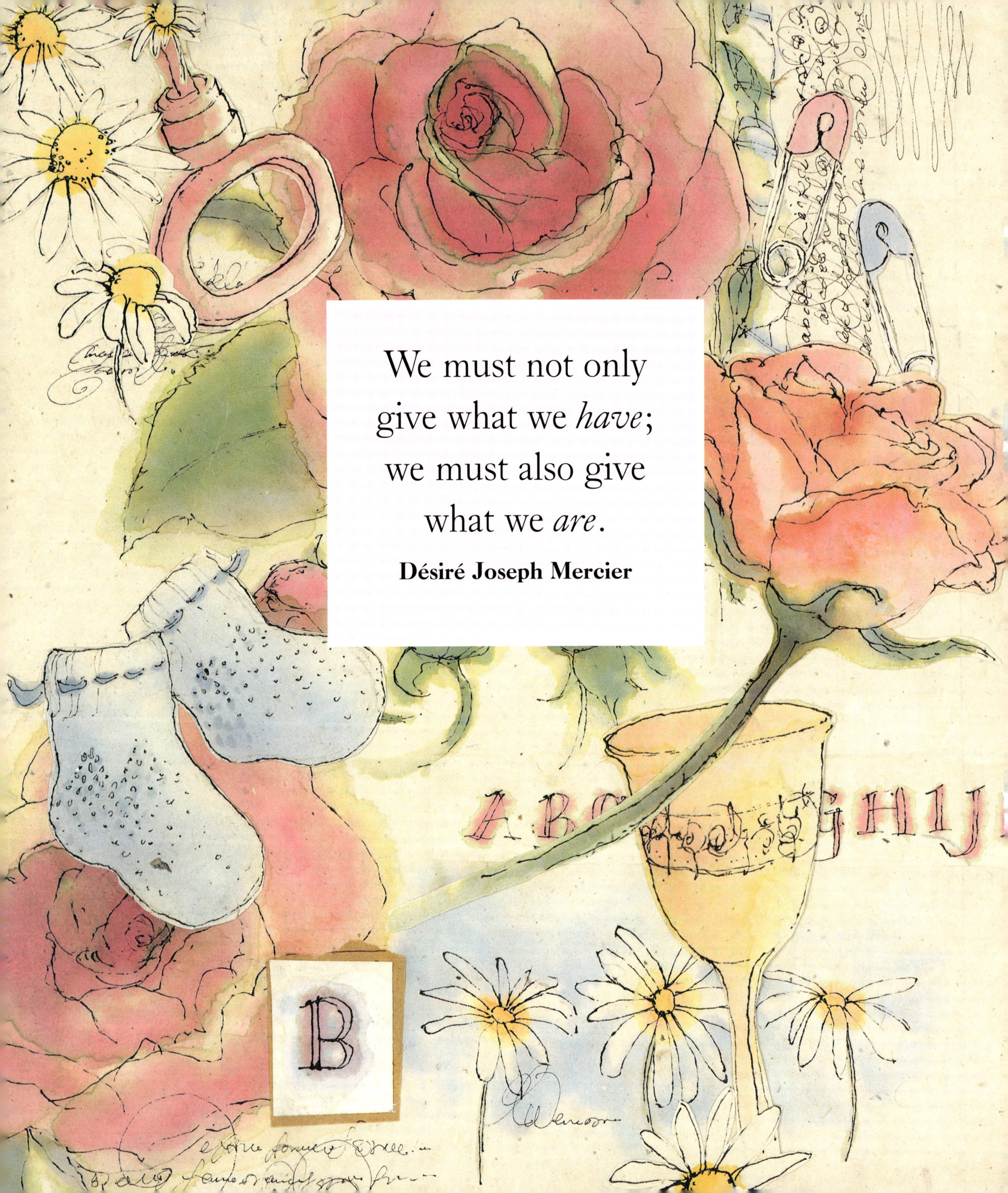

We must not only
give what we *have*;
we must also give
what we *are*.

Désiré Joseph Mercier